Aromatherapy
for Lovers and Dreamers

Also by the Authors
Aromatherapy for Scentual Awareness

Aromatherapy

FOR

Lovers
and
Dreamers

JUDITH WHITE, KAREN DOWNES
& LEON NACSON

Crown Trade Paperbacks ❧ New York

Copyright © 1995 by Judith White, Karen Downes, and Leon Nacson

Published by Crown Trade Paperbacks, 201 East East 50th Street, New York, New York 10022. Member of the Crown Publishing Group.

Random House, Inc. New York, Toronto, London, Sydney, Auckland

http://www.randomhouse.com/

CROWN TRADE PAPERBACKS and colophon are trademarks of Crown Publishers, Inc.

Orginally published in Australia by Nacson and Sons Pty. Ltd. in 1995.

Printed in the United States of America

Design by Cynthia Dunne

Library of Congress Cataloging-in-Publication Data
is available upon request

ISBN 0-517-88667-7 (pbk.)

10   9   8   7   6   5   4   3   2   1

First American Edition

WE DEDICATE THIS BOOK TO OUR BUNDLES OF JOY: JACOB WHITE, JOSHUA WHITE, REBECCA DAY, ELI NACSON, AND RHETT NACSON. MAY THEIR LIVES BE FULL OF LOVERS, DREAMS, AND OF COURSE, MUM AND DAD.

Contents

Acknowledgments

We would like to thank Shanna Provost for her countless hours of research and editing, Leigh Robshaw for her subediting, James Burgin for his invaluable input, and finally, the whole production team, *especially Wendy Hubbert and Patty Eddy,* whose individual creativity honors our humble thoughts.

Introduction

It was a balmy night. The view of Sydney Harbor was spectacular—the lights, the ferries, and the Opera House. Karen, Judith, and I had just finished a very successful exhibition, and we were in a happy, relaxed mood. A number of vaporizers had been lit, and the smell of frankincense, sandalwood, and rose otto permeated the balcony area. The conversation drifted to how we three could combine our knowledge to write a new book that explored the astounding therapeutic qualities of aromatherapy.

Separately, our books had achieved success in their own rights—Karen and Judith's *Aromatherapy for Scentual Awareness,* and my own, *A Dreamer's Guide to the Galaxy.* But we wanted to do a far richer exploration of aromatherapy for intimate relationships and mind expansion. We wanted to do something we felt hadn't been done before. So here it is, *Aromatherapy for Lovers and Dreamers.*

In this new book, we decided to blend the knowledge of modern science with the techniques the ancients employed to enhance their lives and attract their lovers, in order to show how the ancient art of aromatherapy is being validated and used in the twentieth century.

Now we have scientific proof (not that we needed it) that aromatherapy is a healing tool. Scientific data also supports the concept of love chemicals known as *pheromones,* which play an important role in our ability to attract others, especially on the subconscious level.

Anyway, enough scientific talk. In this book you will discover how to romance your body and that of your lover and the importance of touch in healing. You will learn how to create your own individual aromatic blends to use during sensual massage and how to use the oils to maintain the veil of romance.

Aromatherapy
for Lovers and Dreamers

1

Aromatherapy for Me

MY THOUGHT IS ME: THAT IS WHY I CAN'T STOP.
I EXIST BY WHAT I THINK . . . AND I CAN'T
PREVENT MYSELF FROM THINKING.
—JEAN-PAUL SARTRE

Oils Ain't Oils

THE ANCIENTS HAD it, we have it, and we will continue using it all through the day and into the night. In fact, life would be totally boring without it: our sense of smell.

Way back in 4000 B.C., unguents and pomades of aromatic oils were used for anointing kings and holy men. Priests are considered to have been the first retailers of aromatics, dispensing them as perfume as well as for healing purposes.

In past centuries, the Egyptians, Greeks, and Romans used a wide variety of exotic fragrances in their everyday lives. One significant exception to the rule was Julius Caesar. He insisted that his soldiers smell of garlic, so that when they went into battle, the enemy would know the Romans were coming over the hill and definitely not the French!

During the long, cold winters during his siege of Moscow, Napoleon Bonaparte would use up to sixty bottles of rosemary a month to remind him of his beloved Josephine. Rosemary's stimulating effects would also have helped him maintain a clear head. We can't prove it, but if he had added a simple blend of basil and pine to the rosemary, his mental focus would probably have increased, his intuition would have expanded, and he might have realized that the very worst time to try and take over Moscow was during the winter.

It is now an established scientific fact that essential oil aromas affect a person's ability to think and perform tasks more efficiently. The Tokyo construction company Shimuzu uses lemon fragrance in its central air conditioning system to increase productivity in its keypunch operators. This has resulted in a measurable increase in output with far fewer errors.

Just think: in the near future, air infused with lavender and geranium could be piped into New York's notoriously smelly subway system to calm stressed passengers and ease rush-hour aggression. At football matches there could come a time when, to drown out the smell of sweat, hot dogs, and beer, organizers will pump into the stands a blend of lavender, cedarwood and ylang-ylang to relax and calm rival fans.

To encourage more motorists to use cleaner and cheaper fuel, tests were recently run on "perfumed" fuel. The fragrances of Chanel No. 5 and strawberries were two hot favorites. The scented fuel is to be tested in Germany with the goal of introducing it all over

Europe. Imagine cycling in city traffic with the sweet fragrances of orange and lemon hitting your lungs instead of deadly exhaust fumes.

Enough of the future! Today some hospitals and clinics use citrus or woody smells to allay patients' fears and floral oils to relax and calm them. Many aerobics instructors infuse their workout spaces with the scent of lemongrass to help exercisers keep up the pace. In a typical aroma-fitness class, an energizing blend of oils, such as eucalyptus, lemongrass, and rosemary, is sprayed during the vigorous portion of the session; then a more centering and grounding oil like sandalwood is used during the cool-down period.

Some teachers are now looking at ways to incorporate aromatherapy into the classroom. They encourage students to study in the presence of aromatic vapors. Combinations such as lemon, basil, and rosemary have proven very effective. This particular combination promotes focus, alertness, and the ability to absorb information. When the same aromatic combination is reintroduced into an exam environment it helps students recall information with ease from the memory pockets of their brains. The process of association enables the brain to link the aroma perceived with the confidence experienced during previous study sessions.

Nurturing our schoolchildren with the soothing qualities of lavender or the joyous qualities of orange oil is a simple task, achieved with the use of essential oils and a vaporizer. Children can take turns lighting the vaporizer each morning. These "lamp lighters" have the happy responsibility of creating the fragrant environment for the day.

On the Nose

How do we smell? Interesting, after a garlic, onion, and sardine sandwich, but that's not what we mean. The *process* of smelling, in simple terms, begins in the olfactory receptors hidden inside our nose. They're embedded in a small patch of mucous membrane called the *olfactory epithelium,* which is situated high up in the nasal cavity, just below the eyes. This membrane is lined with millions of olfactory nerve cells that are replaced every twenty-eight days.

The cells of the olfactory membrane are, in fact, brain cells. The 80 million or so hairs attached to them carry an enormous amount of information from the environment to the brain. Our sense of smell requires the mere presence of an odor molecule that is registered in the brain when we inhale.

The reason our sense of smell can evoke such powerful memories and emotions is that our olfactory sense is linked directly to the brain's limbic system, one of the most primitive parts of the central nervous system. Fragrant odors pass to the limbic system without being registered by the cerebral cortex. Therefore, even before we are consciously aware we have come in contact with an aroma, our subconscious mind receives and reacts to it. The aroma reaches the innermost control centers of the brain—the headquarters of our sexuality, the impulse of attraction and aversion, our motivation, moods, memory, and creativity.

We store odor memories from the first day of our existence and relate them to specific situations or moods. During our early years, we are trained by those around us to distinguish "good" smells from "bad" smells. Our relationship to smells and aroma is thus learned. Have you ever seen a child step in dog droppings on a path and wonder what on earth all the commotion was about when nearby adults complained loudly about the disgusting smell coming from the shoe? The child doesn't perceive this as a bad or unpleasant smell until he or she associates adults' reactive behavior to the smell.

Smells, moods, and both short- and long-term memory association are all connected and stored in the limbic system, so we can constantly train our nervous system to react to certain situations by using this powerful tool —our sense of smell.

Aromatherapy is effective precisely because we have created individual connections to specific smells. It's like interpreting a dream symbol. We all assign individual interpretations to various symbols. For example, if you ask any number of people what an apple means in a dream, you will get interpretations ranging from forbidden fruit to health. The same goes for the smell of an apple, which could be associated with anything from Mom's apple pie to an old schoolbag.

How many times have you taken an instant dislike to someone and not been sure why? It might have been due to a negative memory in your subconscious, triggered by the combination of their looks, manner, and smell.

Odors trigger our memory all the time. The character Kramer from the television program "Seinfeld" had the right idea. In one episode he came up with the concept of an aftershave called "The Beach," which would automatically transport anyone who smelled it back to those long, lazy days of summer by the ocean.

Food for Thought

Our olfactory senses really come into their own at mealtimes. According to Dr. Susan Schiffman, professor of medical psychology at Duke University, each of us must be olfactorily sated before we actually feel satisfied by a meal.

"Many people are seeking the pleasure of the *odor* of the food," says Schiffman. "The food doesn't tell a person to stop eating; even when they've met their calorie needs, they will go on eating until they have satisfied their hunger for the smell, taste, and texture of food."

Schiffman has been applying this principle to help obese people lose weight. She uses sprays to strengthen the fragrance of food, which creates greater flavor and makes the eater feel satisfied even though less food has been eaten. People who desire sweet foods can reduce their cravings with regular use of the sweet essential oils, such as orange, lemon and bergamot.

Actually, in many cases, when we think

we're enjoying the taste of our food, what we're really enjoying is the aroma. Eighty percent of what we perceive as taste is, in fact, smell. This becomes apparent when our noses are blocked by a cold and even the most delectable pizza tastes like cardboard. Those who suffer from *anosmia* (the inability to distinguish odors) often lose interest in food.

The digestive system is particularly susceptible to smells. The wonderful aroma of essential oils stimulates our appetite and produces digestive juices. Certain oils may even relax a tense stomach. Here is an interesting experiment you can try right away. Before your next big meal, add to your vaporizer a blend of fennel (for its warming and digestive qualities), bergamot, and cedarwood, which will calm and relax you. Notice how this aromatic combination slows you down, deepening your breathing process and, of course, lowering your heart rate. You will find that you consume your meal over a longer period, aiding digestion and, in most cases, eliminating bloating, heartburn, and indigestion.

For a great finishing touch, make your own aromatic after-dinner mint by vaporizing or inhaling the fresh aroma of natural peppermint essential oil.

The Smell of Health

Aromas can affect our sense of well-being. For example, if we have difficulty coming to terms with a new situation, are unable to let go of the past, feel tense, or are unable to experience joy, a new fragrance may help create a fresh mood or impulse. It may help us change our attitude or find a more positive reaction to a given situation. With this in mind, you could add the following essential oils to your medicine cabinet or first aid kit:

Aromatic First Aid Kit

Lavender: For calming the nervous system in tense or anxious moments. Insect bites and stings are quickly relieved by the soothing application of lavender.

Lemongrass: Will diminish anxiety, especially when your muscles feel tight and uncomfortable from nervous tension. This essential oil is especially useful for more robust characters.

Sandalwood: For encouragement, helping you to feel more centered and strong during challenging times. Sandalwood is an ideal oil to use when meditating, as it helps you to reach deep within yourself.

Geranium: For balancing emotional highs and lows, especially when it feels as if you're on a roller-coaster ride in life. Geranium promotes harmonious and friendly conversations.

Frankincense: For releasing fear of moving forward, majestically clearing away emotional debris. Use frankincense to rejuvenate your spirit and realign with your values.

Peppermint: To relieve the symptoms of upset stomach, indigestion, and nausea. Peppermint clears the sinuses and opens the mind for stimulating conversation.

Rosemary: For stimulating the circulation and relieving muscular aches and pains, especially after a long day when there is still that dinner party to attend. Take a soak in a hot rosemary bath to pick up your energy.

Tea tree: The safe and simple first aid in a bottle. The cleansing qualities of tea tree oil enable you to easily address most minor infections. You can care for such superficial irritations as bites, boils, pimples, cuts, and sores with the healing essence of tea tree.

Note: *Essential oils are seventy times more concentrated than the plant or the herb they come from. Be sure to consult chapter 5 for methods of using essential oils.*

Luv That Smell

Instead of someone's reputation preceding them these days, it's usually their perfume or aftershave. Smells from one individual can affect hormone levels in another, so a whole industry has been created to ensure that we put our best pheromones forward.

Pheromones (from the Greek *pher,* "to carry" and *horman,* "to stimulate") are chemicals released by organisms into the environment, where they serve as signals or messages to alter the behavior of other organisms of the same species.

For example, a queen honeybee emanates pheromones in the hive to stimulate congregating, feeding, and grooming behavior by worker bees. Dogs and cats deposit pheromones on outdoor objects to mark their territory. A female dog in heat emits pheromones that male dogs can "smell" from two miles away.

Dr. Michael Stoddart, a zoologist from the University of Tasmania, reported that "human beings are the most highly scented of the great apes." Apparently we possess *apocrine sebaceous glands* at the base of our hair follicles under the arms and especially around the genitals that are activated when we are sexually aroused, frightened, or excited. It is the release of pheromones through these glands—especially in the face—before lovemaking commences that makes kissing such a pleasure.

The existence of these glands suggests that human beings have a well-developed scent communication system, much the same way as animals do. Pheromones may account for us being inexplicably attracted to certain members of the opposite sex. That old saying, "love at first sight," should actually be "love at first smell."

Sigmund Freud considered the repression of smell to be one of the major causes of mental illness and suspected (surprise, surprise) that the nose was related to the sexual organs. To find out for yourself if good ol' Sigmund was on the right track, here are some blends that are designed to stimulate everything from the tip of the nose to the end of the toes.

To cleanse and refresh the body and mind:

Lemongrass	*2 drops*
Rosemary	*5 drops*
Sage	*3 drops*

To tantalize, entice, and arouse the senses:

Sandalwood	*4 drops*
Ylang-ylang	*2 drops*
Neroli	*4 drops*

To deeply relax and bring a meditative state:

Sandalwood	*3 drops*
Frankincense	*5 drops*
Myrrh	*2 drops*

To enhance your intuition and perception:

Pine	*5 drops*
Lavender	*3 drops*
Camomile	*2 drops*

To awaken your body with energy and vitality:

Tea tree	*4 drops*
Peppermint	*2 drops*
Lemon	*4 drops*

To motivate your body for a workout:

Rosemary	*5 drops*
Eucalyptus	*3 drops*
Lemongrass	*2 drops*

To activate your recall and memory:

Rosemary	*5 drops*
Basil	*2 drops*
Lemon	*3 drops*

To promote creativity and humor:

Orange	*5 drops*
Bergamot	*3 drops*
Geranium	*2 drops*

To increase self-esteem and confidence:

Basil	*3 drops*
Sandalwood	*5 drops*
Cypress	*2 drops*

To increase desirability and enthusiasm:

Patchouli	*2 drops*
Orange	*5 drops*
Ylang-ylang	*3 drops*

2

Aromatherapy for Dreamers

WITHIN THE DEPTHS OF OUR SOUL WE HAVE
A SENSE OF WHAT'S POSSIBLE. IT IS THE
SECRETS OF NATURE WHICH MANIFESTS
THE POSSIBILITY.
—JUDITH WHITE

The Sixth Scents—Intuition

WE FIRMLY BELIEVE that every single person is psychic. Some of us choose to work with our innate ability, and others choose to ignore it. Nevertheless, the abilities are there, and if we choose to utilize them, a universe with unlimited possibilities is at our disposal.

Perhaps one of the most important skills to develop for greater psychic awareness is intuition. Business executives have long relied on instinct every time they "go with their gut feeling." And how many times has Sherlock Holmes, Miss Marple, or Hercule Poirot solved the most baffling murder mystery by following a "hunch" or by having complete faith in their intuition? While following the logical path may be great for Mr. Spock, it almost always works out that Captain Kirk's intuition is much more rewarding in the end.

Combined with the use of aromatherapy, intuition can prove even more powerful. Experiencing intuitive insights is not reserved for the seemingly gifted minds of our world; it is an unlimited ability inherent in each and every one of us, and it never runs out. If you feel as if you missed the boat when intuition was being handed out, it's probably just because you've been suppressing or ignoring your natural intuitive capacity. The more you practice using your intuition, the more intuitive you will become. So use it or lose it!

Nobody knows exactly how intuition works, and trying to prove its existence using rational thinking is somewhat paradoxical, perhaps even futile. However, many scientists believe that the left hemisphere of the brain controls rational, analytical, and sequential thought, while the right deals with intuition and creativity. This could explain why many of us seem to have lost our powers of intuition—twentieth-century living means many of us spend our day engaged in activities that exercise the left side of the brain, while activities that use the right side are largely neglected.

Intuition reveals truths that we're not aware of; it's the direct *knowing* of something without the conscious use of reason. You can recognize true intuition because it usually comes as a neutral idea that at first may seem quite matter-of-fact, although compelling. You can distinguish intuition from impulse when the thought hangs around after you've tried to forget it. The best thing to do when you have an intuitive thought is to let it go and wait. If it comes back, let it go again. If it comes back a third time, it's usually safe to follow.

How to Awaken Your Intuition Using Aromatherapy

TAKE TIME TO SMELL THE ROSES

In other words, slow down. You can't very well notice if you're having an intuitive thought when you're running around in a frenzy. It's important to be in the right "head space," which means doing some mental housekeeping every day. Meditation is a good way to clear the cobwebs and put you in touch with your intuitive ability. Here's a great blend to help you take your foot off the pedal, to become more relaxed and at ease.

Centering Blend

Myrrh	2 drops
Sandalwood	5 drops
Frankincense	3 drops

This team of oils will help you center yourself deeply, move surely, and take action with purpose as you go through your day.

SWITCH ON THE ANTENNAE

We all receive intuitive messages in different forms, so it's important to be aware and clear-headed, especially when you're just beginning to work on your intuition. Your intuitions may come as clear visual images, such as in dreams, or they may appear as mental words, sounds, or music that pops into your head. A very clear message could appear on the license plate of a car in front of you. Give your mind a break and pay attention to how you *feel* when you are given a message. The important thing is to remain observant. Before long you'll be able to distinguish patterns that will help you identify true intuitive insights in the future.

To bring more mental clarity and put you in a receptive frame of mind for receiving these signals, try this blend, which stimulates action and focus and activates your memory and retentive ability.

Clearing the Cobwebs

Basil	4 drops
Rosemary	3 drops
Thyme	3 drops

When you clearly identify a moment of intuition, you can "anchor" the moment aromatically. Simply inhale a chosen blend of oils and at the same time hold the clarity of the moment of intuition in your mind. What you think and feel as you smell the oils can be powerfully linked together as an aromatic anchor. Next time you need to be particularly intuitive—for example, when making an important decision—use the same blend to bring back that state of mind.

PRACTICE MAKES PERFECT

Look at your intuition as a regular part of your life, in the same way that you regard eating, sleeping, exercising, making love, etc. Ask yourself empowering questions—ones that require a positive, not a negative, response, and answer them with the first thought that comes into your head. Make quick decisions on minor matters, such as what movie to see or what to eat for dinner. Try to guess who is at the door or on the phone before you answer it. Try to find places without asking directions. Allow the correct information to come to you without trying to work it out by using the logical, left side of your brain.

DEVELOP YOUR TRIGGERS

Become more aware of ways to spark the instinctive aspect of yourself. We suggest that you do this simple exercise using your vaporizer and a favorite essential oil that is in some way symbolic to you—an oil or combination of oils that represents power. Light your vaporizer and add your chosen oil. Begin to visualize something that represents your intuition: a power word or a power object. Inhale deeply and continue to visualize your word or object. Do this for approximately five minutes.

Another great way of effortlessly tapping into your intuition using aromatherapy is by imagining a nature scene and choosing a power fragrance that enhances what you are visualizing while playing soothing music to further engage your senses. Once you have done either of these exercises, it's quite simple to use that fragrance to transport you into that intuitive state. It takes only four seconds for your mind to respond to the aroma and recreate the moment.

CHILL OUT, RELAX, TAKE IT EASY

Most researchers agree that intuitive thoughts come suddenly and characteristically when we're relaxing. Alpha brain waves, which enhance concentration, are more likely to trigger intuition than the rapid beta waves characteristic of ordinary consciousness.

Relaxing in a warm, scented bath induces alpha rhythms and can therefore spark intuition. The bathing temperature is almost as important as the oils you disperse in the water. A warm bath is relaxing, while a hot bath enervates the nervous system. Once your bath is run, indulge yourself by adding the following oils to the water and agitating the surface to disperse the oil molecules.

Bath Blend

Rose otto	*3 drops*
Sandalwood	*3 drops*
Ylang-ylang	*2 drops*

Climb in and take a well-deserved fifteen-minute soak.

Making Scents Out of Sleep

Dreams have consistently played a major role in legends and folklore. Until the twentieth century, dreams were generally believed to be messages from a divine power outside ourselves.

There is a Buddhist legend of a famous dream of Queen Maya, said to be Buddha's mother. Her dream, in which a sacred white elephant entered her body through her side, was interpreted as a prophecy of Buddha's birth. North and South American Indians made exquisite sand paintings and handwoven fabrics depicting dreams. The Indians depended upon their dreams for divine guidance in every facet of their lives—from planting and harvest times to the choice of a mate. The entire Australian aboriginal culture is based on dreaming. Dreamtime legend has been passed from aboriginal elder to initiate since the dawn of time.

We won't go into detail here about what dreams mean, as there are many dream books available that cover the subject adequately. But we will discuss the importance of dreams and how we can nurture them by using aromatic oils.

We all dream. This is a scientific fact. Some people remember their dreams easily, some rarely, and some not at all. But dream we most certainly do.

Every night we enter another level of consciousness—another form of existence where we encounter people, places, and things that we know from our waking reality or that are completely strange to us. During our dreams we escape the usual restraints of time and space. We can be far away in another country, making love to the partner of our fantasies, or even switching from one "life" or "movie script" to another.

Dreaming is an important part of our total existence. If we don't pay attention to our dreams and thought processes, we may risk turning our backs on part of our own individuality. Our experiences during sleep time can provide enlightening information that can help us achieve the highest possible level of personal development. In this way, dreams are an essential part of life.

Aromatherapy can be used as a powerful tool for night dreamers and daydreamers. If you want to use essential oils to facilitate the dreaming process or help you to remember dreams, it's best to use the oils in a vaporizer that is safe for unattended use. Some people deposit their dreamtime drops of essential oil onto a tissue or piece of cotton wool and tuck it into their pillowcase.

Here's something that works for us and almost everyone we have recommended it to:

Mix a blend of oils that is particularly pleasant to you. Perhaps you might like to try some of our recommended blends. Light your vaporizer and let yourself drift off to sleep with the fragrance of the oils lingering in the air. The next morning, as you try to remember your dreams and build your perceptions, vaporize the same blend. The blend you use during your dream state can transport you back to the emotions and visual images of the night before.

The following works particularly well if you want to expand your dream state:

Dreamtime Blend

Clary sage	2 drops
Frankincense	3 drops
Neroli	3 drops

Creating My Dream Lover

Most of us have had dream lovers in one form or another. Remember all those fantasy partners you created when you were a child? By now your dream lovers are probably a lot more sophisticated, and your dreams may be full of erotic or romantic encounters.

Don't worry—having a regular dream lover doesn't mean you're lonely, suppressed, or unfaithful. Nurturing a dream lover can actually help you become more balanced and integrated. We believe that dreams of this type are our higher selves trying to harmonize the aspects of ourselves that become fragmented during our waking life.

If dream lovers appear often in your dreams, it could be a sign that something isn't quite right in your current relationship, or within yourself. It may be a subconscious expression that you are unable to grow or advance any further in life without the right relationship or without attention to certain aspects of your relationships. It doesn't mean you need to start hanging out in singles bars. It just means there is a possibility that some part of your relationship with another or even with yourself isn't meeting all your needs. By expressing this in your dreams, you may be able to work through it.

Just as we attract lovers and partners in our waking life, we believe it is possible to attract dream lovers. If you feel you would like to have a dream lover, as you go to sleep say to yourself, "Tonight I call my dream lover into my dreams." The next morning, use the same blend to help you recall your dreams easily.

Dream Lover Blend

Neroli	3 drops
Ylang-ylang	3 drops
Sandalwood	2 drops

Sleep on It

We spend so much time in our beds, but we rarely think about the environment we've created there. A good night's sleep depends on feeling safe and peaceful when you lay your head on your pillow. Nurture yourself! Consider surrounding your body with natural-fiber bed linen. You deserve it.

Fresh air is important, so try to get as much of it circulating in the bedroom as possible. And of course, a large bed is important when sleeping with someone else, to allow for different sleeping patterns.

Watch what you eat before sleeping. Throughout the day, your body moves through cycles: absorption, assimilation, and elimination. At night the body assimilates the nutrients from the food that it has absorbed throughout the day, so go easy on the evening meal, especially after 8:00 P.M. Mental and emotional conditions also affect the quality of sleep. Do things that relax you before you jump into bed. Just as a reminder, here are some great blends to help you "punch out some z's."

Sleepmakers

BLEND #1

Patchouli	2 drops
Lavender	2 drops
Marjoram	4 drops

BLEND #2

Sandalwood	2 drops
Orange	4 drops
Marjoram	2 drops

BLEND #3

Marjoram	2 drops
German Camomile	3 drops
Neroli	3 drops

BLEND #4

Lavender	3 drops
Orange	3 drops
Marjoram	2 drops

Daydream Believers

Daydreaming, sometimes called "reverie," is the most common use of our imagination. It takes no effort to daydream—we merely let our imagination walk hand in hand with our memories. Daydreams, reveries, and fantasies are unlike sleeping dreams because they are under our conscious control. Therefore we can use aromatherapy to turn these positive visualizations into creative tools for positive change.

In his book *You'll See It When You Believe It,* Wayne Dyer says that virtually everything we do is a result of the pictures we place in our minds before making the attempt. However, to manifest what we truly desire, we must be willing to do *anything* it takes to make it happen.

Here are some practical steps for creative daydreaming. Set a time and place to daydream. Pick what feels like the best time of day for you. Some people are more creative early in the morning, before the hustle and bustle begins. Others find they are more creative and relaxed at sunset or late at night.

Find out when your creative juices flow most intensely and make an appointment with yourself. Think about it. We make appointments with our doctors, dentists, and plumbers, but when was the last time you made an appointment with yourself?

Set up a sanctuary where you will not be interrupted, such as a bedroom, a study, or even out in nature—somewhere that inspires you. Have your chosen blend vaporizing for a while before you enter to allow the aromatic energy to build up.

Get into a comfortable position. Breathe in the aromatic blend. Allow your daydreaming to begin. You may want to create a better lifestyle, develop a new career, find a new lover, or increase your material possessions. Remember, creative thought is very powerful, and there is every chance that you will create what you want in your life.

If your mind wanders for a while during the process, that's okay. Become the observer and see where it goes, as your subconscious may be trying to tell you something. When you feel it's appropriate, let the daydream go—forget about it and rejoin the "land of the living."

The best essential oils to stimulate creative daydreams are clary sage, orange, sandalwood, and rose otto. As a team, these oils will promote a sense of euphoria, purity, and nobility, at the same time fostering an open and generous heart.

Meditation Makes Good Scents

Meditation is different from daydreaming in that its purpose is not to orchestrate thoughts but to clear the mind. By watching our thoughts and setting them free, we can reach a deeper perspective of ourselves.

Set a time and place to meditate. A popular time to meditate is before sunrise, as this is when "thought space" is relatively serene. Or you may decide to meditate before you go to sleep to release the thoughts that have built up during the day.

Set up a sanctuary where you will not be interrupted—somewhere that inspires you. Many people prefer to meditate in nature, while others set up a meditation room. It's important to meditate at the same time and place each day to build up energy and promote a clear transmission to your higher consciousness.

Choose a time when you won't be disturbed. Place a desired aromatic blend in a vaporizer. You may play inspiring music or use a guided visualization tape if you are new to meditation.

Sit in a comfortable position, making sure your spine is straight. Start to breathe deeply. Follow the breath as it fills your lungs. Focus either on a mantra (a neutral word or phrase) or visualize your breath in a certain color. Repeat the mantra over and over in your mind to maintain focus.

If a thought comes to you, don't try to push it away; simply observe it and let it pass. If the same thought keeps coming back, it may represent an issue that you need to examine or resolve. Vaporize essential oils that help release anxiety and recurring negative thoughts, such as bergamot, frankincense, ylang-ylang, rose otto, and orange.

Creative Fantasies

We all have innermost desires and fantasies that we rarely disclose. By taking time to indulge in and explore these intimate secrets without shame, you will be amazed at what you discover about yourself. Fantasizing can often assist you in self-discovery, which can ultimately be of great benefit in a relationship, should you choose to share these secrets and desires with your partner.

Most psychologists agree that sexual fantasy is an essential part of life and can be used in a positive way to heal the psyche. To explore the hidden depths of your greatest desires, to delve deep into your secret wishes, or to be more creative with your own body expression, explore your fantasies—they can be an exciting way of awakening your sensual awareness. Here's what we suggest:

Fantastic Fantasy

Clary sage	*2 drops*
Ylang-ylang	*2 drops*
Neroli	*4 drops*

Yoga, meditation, or a relaxing massage before sleep will all prepare the body and soul for its nocturnal journeying. Of course, another way to relax the body and mind is to make love. Sharing the natural energies of life is a form of communion that clears the mind and restores the body. Time spent in bed just before sleep holding someone you love can be the most precious moment of the day.

If your day has been particularly busy or difficult and your mind is spinning with thoughts as you hop into bed, play classical or peaceful music, burn a Sleepmaker Blend (see p. 34) in your vaporizer, and breathe slowly and deeply.

Another great way to prepare the mind for sleep is to turn it backward, visually tracing every thought of the day. For example, picture yourself getting into bed, then having a warm shower to prepare for bed, then switching off the television, then sitting down to watch television, then having dinner, then arriving home from work, then driving in traffic, etc., until you see yourself getting out of bed that morning.

This process allows the mind to release extraneous impressions, thoughts, and memories that clutter the brain. If you feel an emotion about a particular event, replay the scene in your head and say, "Oh, I see I'm feeling angry about that." Then let it go. If you can't get past a particular emotional event, you may decide to talk to someone about it the next day. For immediate benefit, draw a picture about how you feel, write down your feelings in your journal, or tell yourself you will resolve the issue in your dreams.

Taking control of your creative process through dreams, daydreaming, and positive creative fantasies will leave you space to create the perfect loving environment for yourself and your partner.

Don't Worry, Be Happy

One of the greatest destroyers of a good night's sleep is anxiety. It's that feeling of unease, worry, and tension about what *may* happen—the feeling that wells up in the pit of your stomach and ruins your whole day—and night.

Although it seems as if tomorrow's dinner party, next week's interview, or next month's presentation are contributors to this anxiety, they're not. The real cause of anxiety is our thoughts. As Shakespeare said, "There is nothing either good or bad, but thinking makes it so."

Thoughts like "What will they think of me?," "What if I forget the words?," or "What if I say something stupid?" all increase feelings of anxiety. What lies behind most of these thoughts is fear of the unknown. It is always fear of what you *think* may happen that ties your stomach up in knots. To free yourself from anxiety, you have to take responsibility for your internal thoughts—*you* are the originator of the thinking. Choose words and concepts that empower rather than imprison you.

Set aside some time to consider your challenges. Think about them rationally, visualizing positive things that may happen rather than expecting the worst. Confide in someone you trust, and see if they can offer some word of wisdom or lend a sympathetic ear. Every challenge has a solution; it's just a matter of finding it.

While you're searching for that elusive solution, which is probably just around the corner, you can use aromatherapy to help calm your nerves and promote a feeling of relaxation.

Here are some blends to use when you're feeling anxious or worried.

Stressbusters

BLEND #1

Basil	2 drops
Bergamot	3 drops
Lavender	3 drops

BLEND #2

Orange	2 drops
Bergamot	3 drops
Cedarwood	5 drops

BLEND #3

Lavender	3 drops
Cedarwood	4 drops
Orange	3 drops

BLEND #4

Sandalwood	3 drops
Patchouli	2 drops
Orange	5 drops

Be Happy, Don't Worry

What is happiness? Well, it's difficult to say, since everyone's idea of happiness is so different. Webster's Dictionary defines happy as "enjoying or characterized by well-being or contentment." The noted nineteenth-century philosopher/psychologist William James believed happiness is reflected in the ratio of one's accomplishments to one's aspirations. Some say it's the measure of positive against negative experiences.

While we all have different ideas of what constitutes a positive experience, most of us know when one comes along, and the resulting feeling of happiness is easily recognized. The general consensus of current research is that to be happier, we need to take pleasure in the little things in life rather than waiting for the big bonanzas. The emphasis should be on frequency, rather than intensity. Becoming truly happy could be as simple as finding out what it is that makes you happy and doing it as often as possible.

Personal control is one of the most important factors to consider in looking for happiness, particularly with regard to the creation of positive and negative experiences in our lives. To some degree, it is the feeling that we've made something good happen in our lives that produces a feeling of happiness. It gives us the sense that we have mastery over our lives. It is generated from within.

While healthy relationships, a rewarding career, financial strength, or material possessions may impart a feeling of happiness, it's important to realize that *we* are the source of our own happiness, rather than constantly looking to external stimuli. The world's greatest thinkers, philosophers, and religious leaders have all understood that happiness lies within. The happiness that can be achieved by those who meditate for many years is often described as "bliss." It is a feeling of being completely happy for no reason at all other than just *being* and connecting with one's spirituality.

In the meantime, creating many opportunities to feel good in our lives is a sure way to achieve happiness. These events may be as simple as listening to a beautiful piece of music, watching a glorious sunset, strolling on the beach, or working in the garden.

Louise L. Hay, author of the best-seller *Heal Your Body,* tells us she loves to use essential oils when traveling because the fragrances transport her back to her wonderful garden. "I feel automatically rested and relaxed," says Louise. "It gives me a feeling of being back in nature."

On a physiological level, essential oils can help us feel happier, uplifting our spirits and helping us think more positively. We'd love to suggest a universal "happy blend" that could be used by everyone, but as we've said, happiness is a very individual feeling. It's important to use your own judgment in choosing the oils that appeal to you most. It can be great fun experimenting with oils to find the blends that give you the biggest lift.

To get you on the right track, here are some blends that never fail to make us feel on top of the world.

Uplifters

BLEND #1

Orange	4 drops
Clary sage	2 drops
Ylang-ylang	3 drops

BLEND #2

Patchouli	3 drops
Orange	4 drops
Clary sage	3 drops

BLEND #3

Lemon	3 drops
Orange	3 drops
Bergamot	4 drops

BLEND #4

Bergamot	4 drops
Lemon	3 drops
Lemongrass	3 drops

BLEND #5

Orange	*4 drops*
Ylang-ylang	*3 drops*
Frankincense	*3 drops*

BLEND #6

Clary sage	*5 drops*
Patchouli	*2 drops*
Vetiver	*3 drops*

3

Aromatherapy for Lovers

SEX IS ONE OF THE NINE REASONS FOR
REINCARNATION . . . THE OTHER EIGHT
ARE UNIMPORTANT.
—HENRY MILLER

SEXUALITY IS OUR primal response to
nature, without which we would not sur-
vive as a species. Without maintaining and
honoring the vital role sex plays in our
lives, we would literally disappear off the
planet! The sexual act heralds us into this
existence.

Smell is the first of our senses to come

into being, closely followed by touch. We touch other people to communicate affection, we touch ourselves to continually embrace our own identity, giving ourselves a sense of reassurance and certainty, a sense of connectedness. This is often the reason people seek out sexual gratification—to simply feel connected to another person and to get in touch with yet another dimension of themselves. To give love and be loved is ultimately what we all desire.

When we are infants, the loving touch of our parents reassures us that we are accepted and helps us to grow up with a feeling of self-worth. In early childhood we instinctively associate touch with love, comfort, and affection.

Our receptors for touch are located in the skin, including the lips, tongue, eyes, nose, genitals, and scalp, with each part possessing varying degrees of sensitivity. You and a partner can help each other reclaim or strengthen your natural capacity to give and receive pleasure through the use of sensual, loving touch.

Going All the Way

Touching and caressing should play a major role in lovemaking. Prolonged fondling and caressing stimulates the body's sexual hormones and heightens arousal, increasing energetic charge and sensory fulfillment. Add to this the power of aromatic essences and the stimulation of the senses that they bring, and you can learn to reach new heights of ecstasy.

Touch alone can be a satisfying experience, and being sensually aroused does not necessarily have to lead to intercourse. An intimate and prolonged sensual experience can be valuable for both partners for those times when either one may not want to "go all the way." There is real magic to be found in your relationship when you spend time exploring each other's bodies apart from actually making love.

If you're tired, stressed, or feel you've given all you can for one day, nonconditional caressing can play a nurturing role. A gentle stroking and caressing with no expectation or agenda can, in a caring and honoring way, motivate and inspire lovemaking.

Many people find the experience of being caressed for an extended period even more intimate than lovemaking, and may need to accustom themselves gradually to these new dimensions of pleasure. To reach new heights of ecstasy, let your body surrender to the loving touch of your partner.

To enhance the mood and raise the spirits of both partners, consider the following blends, which are ideal in a massage base oil of 1 ounce (20 ml.). You could also add them to your vaporizer:

Mood Setters

BLEND #1

Clary sage	3 drops
Sandalwood	3 drops
Ylang-ylang	4 drops

BLEND #2

      Ylang-ylang   *3 drops*
      Patchouli   *2 drops*
      Orange   *5 drops*

BLEND #3

      Neroli   *4 drops*
      Sandalwood   *3 drops*
      Rose otto   *3 drops*

Honoring Rhythms

No matter how much we love our partners, sometimes we have more enthusiasm for intimacy than others. Levels of intimacy can rise and fall dramatically without this being any reflection on the quality of the relationship.

We each experience personal rhythms on the mental, physical, and emotional levels. Rhythms have high, low, and critical points each month, and depending on the position of these rhythms, we may feel tired or energetic, emotionally strong or weak, mentally dull or acute.

You can make use of the essential oils to help balance your emotional rhythms. Couples can learn to maintain a more balanced interaction, rather than being on an emotional and physical roller coaster, by using carefully chosen blended oils. The following blend can balance even the most charged moment.

Balancing Blend

Geranium	3 drops
Cedarwood	2 drops
Orange	5 drops

Remember, it is important to choose essential oils to first enhance the way *you* want to be. You may think at times that your partner needs help more than you do. When this happens, take your observations personally and make a blend up for yourself. When you make a change, so will everything else.

Extinguishing an Old Flame

Though we may soon forget things we see and hear, we remember odors for a lifetime. We've discussed how the staying power of the sense of smell can work in our favor, but sometimes an ex-lover's perfume or aftershave can bring back memories of a relationship that you would prefer to forget.

Here's how to cleanse your "scents" memory of an unwanted association. First, find a quiet, peaceful place and relax. Fill the room with the aroma that you want to eradicate. Once you feel relaxed and safe, breathe in the aroma deeply. Then use the cleansing blend described below and allow it to overpower the scent you want to erase. As the aroma you want to get rid of slowly disappears, visualize the associated person, place, or event disappearing with it, fading away until there's no trace of it in your memory via imagery or smell.

Cleansing Blend

Eucalyptus	*3 drops*
Frankincense	*2 drops*
Lemon	*3 drops*

Just as we can each have our own aromatic signature, so too can a relationship. Each loving relationship is different—we make love in different ways to different people, we enjoy different pastimes together, go to new and different places, and discover new foods and restaurants that we haven't shared with anyone else in just this way.

It's a good idea to set a unique imprint on each new relationship. This will consist of your stamp of personal aromas plus those perfumes favored by both of you, coupled with the particular smells of the environments in which you make love.

You may want to consider changing the aromatic energy after each relationship to make way for a new romantic adventure. Changing perfumes with each new lover, making up new blends for massage oils, lingerie, and bed linen, will pave the way for a unique relationship based on the present moment—without subconscious aromatic hangovers from the past.

Sensual Bathing

Water plays a sustaining and purifying role in our life. It is a powerful agent of purification for the body and mind. Although natural body odors are stimulants for sex, some people still feel more comfortable coming together squeaky clean. Racing off to bathe after sex, however, is considered a no-no, as the perspiration produced by bodies making love contains subtle minerals and vital secretions that are beneficial if absorbed.

A luxurious bath scented with aromatic oils in a warm room with subdued lighting is your second sanctuary—your place to get away from the world. For many sensual romancers —from now on we'll call them "aromancers" —the bathroom is almost as sacred a space as the bedroom. It is here that you can incorporate ritual into your lovemaking by making bathing an erotic first step in your love play.

When bathing either alone or with a partner, it's important to set the scene. Make sure there are no drafts and that you will not be disturbed. Fill the room with candles and make sure they are close at hand so that you can blow them out intermittently as you soak. Play your favorite peaceful music to set the mood. Choose your favorite aromatic blend and add a few drops to the warm (not hot) water.

If you're after a night of hot passion and much physical activity, don't spend too long in a warm bath, as it is very relaxing and can easily lead to drowsiness—unless, of course, you choose to make love in the bath. In that case spend as long as you like. Bath size permitting, you can use the extra buoyancy to assist you and your partner in achieving more complex lovemaking positions.

If you're bathing alone, choose oils to uplift your tired body and clear your mind, or those designed to relax and release anxiety and stress. Lying in the bath for an hour is the perfect way to heal yourself and the ideal place to give yourself the gift of self-pleasuring.

On Your Mark, Get Scented, Go

Preparing for the ritual of lovemaking together by sharing an exotic bath is the ultimate erotic experience, but it's not possible in all situations. If you know you have a night of lovemaking ahead and want to present yourself to your lover in an appealing way, or if you simply want to pamper your body yourself, use the following blend.

The Seducer

Neroli	3 drops
Ylang-ylang	4 drops
Rose otto	3 drops

After a luxurious bath, take a small blending bowl and pour in 1 ounce of jojoba oil. Add your essential oils. Take a small amount and smooth the aromatic blend over your body, paying attention to all areas. If you want to arouse the senses even more, concentrate on massaging the inner thighs and whole pelvic girdle gently. Of course, if your partner is available to rub the oil in for you, even better! Remember, show and tell your partner how to do the massage that you like, choosing encouraging words to express your romantic instruction.

Sensual Massage

Sensual massage is one of the most wonderful ways of ensuring a memorable encounter. It is important to set the scene before a sensual massage.

Sensual Massage Checklist

- Are your hands smooth to the touch? You can remove dry, chapped skin with a fine-grained emery board.

- Are your nails short, clean, and smooth?

- Have you taken off any jewelry to avoid scratching your partner?

- Is your bedding appropriate? A cotton mattress such as a Japanese-style futon or layers of blankets placed on the floor make a good surface to provide a massage.

- Do you have lots of soft, fluffy towels or a cotton blanket handy to place over the parts of the body not being massaged? This will allow your partner to relax further.

- Do you have everything you need within reach? This is to avoid losing contact with the body and breaking the flow of the massage.

- Do you have candles, soft music, warm lighting, fresh flowers, and aromatic blends to contribute to the ambience?

Remember, massage is not a replacement for foreplay. Giving a loving massage to your partner must be kept for an entirely separate occasion from giving a sensual massage as part of your foreplay activities. It is of the utmost importance in order to maintain trust and honor in your relationship that you discuss which type of massage you are partaking in before you begin. Sensual massage doesn't always have to lead to intercourse. It is a loving gesture to offer your partner an intimate massage with no strings attached, so he or she can fully experience the joy of receiving.

Before beginning your massage, it is a good idea to warm your blended oil. Once you have made your blend in a small glass bowl, place it in a larger bowl of hot water to warm it a little. Alternatively, you can use a heat source like a candle to heat the bowl so that your oil stays warm throughout the massage. Cold oil on warm skin may shock your partner and break the mood, so try a little on your fingers first to test the temperature.

It's also important to remember to create an equal balance in the body when massaging. Don't massage just one hand or foot and leave the other unattended, and don't stimulate one side of the body without stimulating the corresponding parts on the other side.

Sensual Massage Blend

Rose otto	3 drops
Patchouli	2 drops
Clary sage	2 drops
Sandalwood	3 drops

Add these essential oils to one ounce of high-quality massage base oil, like olive or jojoba. Oil each part of the body before you begin massaging it. Use enough oil to allow your hands to glide easily and sensuously over your partner's body without creating friction. Remember, massage oil nourishes the skin. Any oil massaged onto the skin will be absorbed.

Sensuous massage requires a gentle touch, so if the receiver is sensitive in a particular area, lightly rub with nurturing, gentle strokes. As the giver, this is your opportunity to express selfless, unconditional love to your partner, so do your best to clear your mind of all thoughts concerning your own sexual gratification and dedicate yourself purely to giving.

Keep your breathing slow, deep, regulated, and in synchronization with your partner's. No strain or great energy is required in a sensual massage. Make sure that the point from which you move is instigated by the energy in the lower abdomen. Use a flowing, feather-light touch, as if skimming your palms over water. By moving your hands lightly in this way, you will direct the flow of energy toward the sexual center. As you do this, your partner may experience a heightened sensual enjoyment in the lower abdomen and genitals. Get him or her to breathe into this energy and allow it to flow to all parts of the body.

If you feel yourself or your partner becoming too excited, stop for a moment and rest your hands lightly on his or her body. When your partner feels ready to continue, do so gently. It is natural for humans to experience body sensations, and it is an acquired and rewarding skill to be able to experience them without having to release them externally from the body.

To *receive* a sensual massage requires nothing more than the willingness to accept and enjoy the pleasure that your partner gives you without having to do anything in return. Your ability to relinquish control to your partner will, to a large extent, govern your capacity to receive pleasure. Be ready to accept the form or the pattern that the massage takes and surrender to the experience by breathing deeply and gently and focusing on the part of your body being touched.

Once the massage is completed, wipe any excess oil off gently with a soft towel and then, well . . . that's up to you.

Your Feet Don't Stink

A tender foot massage not only awakens sensuality, it can also be very therapeutic. In

Oriental medicine and reflexology, it is believed that the organs in the body are connected by "meridians" to specific areas of the foot. By applying gentle pressure and rubbing in a circular motion, you can send healing to specific parts of your own or your partner's body. The instep and ankle area of the foot are erogenous zones, so if you are both in the mood for adventure, concentrate on these areas. Avoid using too much pressure in foot massage, or you could stimulate uncomfortable side effects. Don't forget that the purpose of sensuous massage is always to expand the pleasure of our sense of touch.

Foot Massage Blend

Peppermint	1 drop
Basil	2 drops
Bergamot	2 drops
Base massage oil	2 teaspoons (10 ml.)

Erotic Massage

While sensual massage is ideal for building trust and intimacy between partners, erotic massage is designed to lift the sexual relationship to even loftier heights. Many partners find it impossible to experience such high levels of ecstasy without seeking some kind of sexual completion, making erotic massage the ultimate kind of foreplay.

The most influential sexual organ in the body is the mind, and this is where aromatherapy enters the picture. By using the right blends to stimulate our bodies and minds, we can set the stage for some very steamy "scentual" encounters.

Scent works mainly on the instinctive centers, stimulating our basic primal urge: sexual excitement. When preparing for an erotic massage, we recommend that you choose oils that align with the smell of human sexual hormones and pheromones, such as the base notes. Oils such as sandalwood, vetiver, cedarwood, and rose otto are very arousing. We know of one couple who created a special aromatic link to their lovemaking by having rose otto at hand at the point of orgasm, at which time they deeply inhaled this arousing fragrance. Can you imagine their connection to this aroma following this experience?

During massage, both the giver and receiver can benefit from the aromatic energy created by essential oils and the natural body odors they have stimulated during the massage.

Your touch can be a little firmer during erotic massage, although starting out with light, titillating strokes will build your partner to a higher level of ecstasy. You must always rely on feedback from your partner when giving an erotic massage, respecting their wishes to stop at any time.

Don't limit yourself to using your hands during erotic massage. Get creative—there are lots of ways to get a grip on the situation! To help, we've listed the most erotic blend that we could come up with and still guarantee your safety. Speaking of safety, just a quick note on safe sex. Remember, *if it's not on, it's not on!*

Erotica Blend

Rose otto	*2 drops*
Neroli	*2 drops*
Patchouli	*1 drop*
Ylang-ylang	*3 drops*

The Healing Power of Sex

We don't think anyone reading this book will disagree that during those times when we have a fulfilling sex life, the positive vibrations tend to spill over into the rest of our life. Healthy sex promotes a feeling of well-being and contentment. Good sex with a caring partner can increase our self-esteem, helping us to feel better about ourselves in general. The physical and emotional release can also help reduce depression and anxiety.

Making love in the morning can put you in a good mood for the whole day. Coming home after a busy day at work and having a satisfying sexual experience can help you relax and unwind.

Not only can sex help heal us on an emotional and psychological level, there's also evidence of a strong connection between sex and the immune system. In other words, the various elements of sex, including arousal, desire, excitement, intimacy, and physical release, may enhance the immune system's ability to ward off illness. An apple a day may keep the doctor away, but a *grapple* a day could be a lot more exciting!

A good frolic can also be a natural pain reliever, and there are many reports of people who get relief through sexual activity from menstrual cramps, arthritis, and migraine.

The Healing Power of Abstinence

Men and women can be sensuous and sexual even if they're not in a sexual relationship with a partner. At different times in our lives we may choose to abstain from sex for a while or we may find ourselves without a partner. This doesn't mean we have to relinquish our sexuality for the duration. In this day and age, some of the most sensuous people will go through periods of celibacy from time to time. These can be healing times when we hold our sexual energy within and use it to enhance our creativity.

Celibacy is not about denial, and it certainly doesn't mean we can't enjoy the healing energy of orgasms. In fact, many people, especially women, discover more about their bodies and their sexual desires when they are without a partner and left alone to gratify their inner yearnings. If you choose to be celibate, it can give you the space and time to discover what it is you really need in a sexual relationship.

It's important to nurture your body and soul at those times when you are celibate. Give yourself time out, indulge your senses in things that make you feel special. To maintain your sensuality, wear sensuous clothes made of materials that feel comforting against the skin. Smooth oils and moisturizers over your body and hair regularly, sleep in sensuous bed linen, and set the energy in your bedroom and sanctuary just as lovers do.

It's probably wise not to wear a lot of aphrodisiac aromas when you're choosing to be celibate. Try something light and fruity, like orange and bergamot, or warm, like cedarwood and sandalwood.

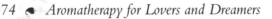

4

Aromatherapy
Blends for
Lovers,
Dreamers,
and Me

LOVE LOOKS NOT WITH THE EYES,

BUT WITH THE MIND:

AND THEREFORE IS

WING'D CUPID PAINTED BLIND.

—WILLIAM SHAKESPEARE

WHEN THE ANCIENT aromancers produced
perfumes, they used only essential oils. As

time went on, the art of distillation was invented. Alcohol was soon found to be an inexpensive extender of fragrance that at the same time seemed to have a preserving quality.

The popularity of diluted perfumes swept Europe, where many soon preferred them to pure concentrates made with only essential oils.

Now, in the 1990s, we are turning back to what was instinctively known by our ancestors: the integrity of plants in their natural state is truly a reflection and embodiment of our own natural selves. We are returning to our intuitive nature, using aromatherapy and the alchemy of blending pure plant oils to enhance the qualities of who we are and what we feel.

Aroma-Self

If you want to create a perfume that enhances your character, use the principle of likeness. Your personalized blend can be a reflection of who you are in the world, the qualities that are important to you, or the qualities that you wish to enhance.

One soft-spoken woman told us how she had always avoided going to parties. She felt awkward trying to communicate over the music and loud chatter. So she created an aromatic blend to enhance bold, enthusiastic, and energetic conversation. Orange, clary sage, and sandalwood were her choices. They helped her to focus on having a great time socially with her husband and friends.

If you want to create a perfume that enhances your character, use the principle of "likeness." The perfume you create should not be in opposition to your character type. For example, an outgoing person should use a blend of oils that signify the extrovert personality, such as the uplifting quality of bergamot, the exuberance of orange, the stimulating nature of rosemary, or the vitality of peppermint. A more introverted person may wish to project the serenity of lavender, the calm of cedarwood, or the strength of sandalwood.

You can also create blends to signify differing moods. Aromatic oils with light, fresh fragrances may be worn during the day, while more subtle, feminine fragrances are more suitable for evening.

Another goal of therapeutic aromatherapy can be to balance the masculine/feminine within each of us. We can do this with essential oils, as each particular oil carries an energy that is the intrinsic nature and vibration of the plant.

In Eastern traditions, all natural forces are divided into two categories: passive (or negative) and active (or positive), called respectively yin and yang. The forces of yin and yang interplay continually within nature and human beings. Yin, for example, is exhibited in the *passive, gentle, slow, female, dark,* and *earthly,* while yang is *active, strong, fast, male, light,* and *heavenly.* Yin meridians flow up the body, while yang flow down it.

Eastern philosophy also categorizes people into yin or yang types, even though our characters usually express different aspects of each.

Here are some oils you can use to help balance your personal yin/yang energies:

Yin Oils

Sage	Lavender
Orange	Camomile, German
Eucalyptus	Vetiver
Peppermint	Ylang-ylang
Camomile, Roman	Rose
Geranium	Cypress

Yang Oils

Basil	Rosemary
Bergamot	Fennel
Cedarwood	Juniper
Lemongrass	Clary sage
Lemon	Sandalwood
Tea tree	Patchouli
Marjoram	Myrrh
Thyme	Neroli
Pine	Frankincense

Most perfume bases contain alcohol, but you can use jojoba oil as an alternative base.

Jojoba is a natural fluid wax, not an oil, and has a life span of ten years. Jojoba will suspend your essential oils and help preserve your natural aromatic perfumes.

It's a good idea to keep differing strengths of a favorite blend on hand for varying uses. You may use a light blend, similar in intensity to an eau de cologne, during the day. Your day blend might embrace the citrus family, as these scents are light and refreshing. A stronger perfume blend is appropriate for the evening. This blend might include the wood or root oils like sandalwood or vetiver.

Eau de cologne has the smallest amount of essential oil—3 percent in a 70 percent alcohol base. Perfume requires 20 drops of essential oil in a base of 1 ounce of jojoba oil.

Once you have mixed a perfume blend, let it rest for two to three weeks to allow it to ripen like fine wine.

Always keep your oils in dark-colored glass. You may wish to purchase fancy miniature bottles of differing dark colors to signify different blends. Keep the lids tight, as essential oils are volatile. They will evaporate quickly when exposed to the air.

Remember that the same perfume may smell different on different people. If a fragrance appears too strong, dilute it with jojoba oil or alcohol. If it is too light, add a few more drops of essential oil to the blend.

Hitting the Right Note

When it comes to blending, expert perfumers around the world have developed a system that can be applied both to aromatics and to fragrance combinations. Using this system, each of the essential oils is referred to as a *note*, which when blended is called a *chord*. Three different notes are used to categorize the essential oils. If we were to look at these notes in terms of our own human qualities, they might appear like this:

TOP NOTE

These are the partygoers. Their exuberance and lightheartedness make them the first ones you notice in a crowd. They have a strong impact initially but not much staying power. These oils love to jump out of the bottle and give the first impression of a fragrance. They evaporate quickly.

Top notes include sage, orange, eucalyptus, peppermint, basil, bergamot, lemongrass, lemon, and tea tree.

MIDDLE OR HEART NOTES

These are the mediators in life, the diplomats who hold council before jumping in. They are the balancing influence between any extremes, whether heightened activity, excessive frivolity, or too much seriousness. These oils are the heart of a fragrance. They balance a blend to make it more rounded.

Middle notes include Roman Camomile, German Camomile, lavender, geranium, marjoram, thyme, pine, rosemary, fennel, juniper, and clary sage.

BASE NOTES

These are the stabilizers in life, the dependable notes that will always be there to support and hold down the fort. They possess a deep, reliable calm. Top notes need these anchoring elements to keep things together. Base note oils are used as fixatives to prolong a perfume's presence.

Base notes include sandalwood, vetiver, ylang-ylang, rose, cypress, patchouli, myrrh, neroli, frankincense, and cedarwood.

Aromancing is based largely on intuition. Let your nose guide you. If you worry too much about balancing top, middle, and base notes, you may miss the experience of creating a blend that is perfect for you.

When you start out, begin with simple mixtures. It's fun to just experiment for a while, blending the essential oils and leaving them in a bowl to ripen before adding them to base mixtures, or diffusing them in a vaporizer to see how you feel about the blend over time.

Some essential oils are particularly suitable

for beginners because they may be combined with nearly all other oils. These include lavender, bergamot, cedarwood, orange, sandalwood, and rosemary.

Certain essential oils blend more easily than others. When making your own perfume, you may feel that the heart note in the mixture has become too pronounced. Add an essential oil that has both a top and a middle note, such as orange or geranium.

When blending, first decide on the mood you're trying to reflect. Then organize your oils —no more than three, so you don't confuse your nose. (If you inhale too many aromas at any one time, you will find you are not able to differentiate between them after a while.

Choose an area free from other strong aromas and make sure the room is warm and free from drafts. Until you can identify aromas without knowing what they are, write their names on strips of blotting paper and dip the ends of the strips into the oil. Hold the paper about an inch from your nose, careful not to touch the skin, and sniff.

It's a good idea to keep a diary of your work. Describe the aroma (woody, light, fruity, etc.), then write down the effect it has on your mind and emotions.

It may take some experimenting to balance your blends in satisfying aromas. You will quickly find out which oils overpower others, but in a good blend, components will complement each other.

Top Tips

- Bergamot always enhances the fragrance of other essential oils. It is often used in eau de cologne.

- Geranium is often used to complement or replace rose otto.

- Citrus oils shouldn't be worn on the skin in the presence of ultraviolet light.

- Always dilute essential oils before applying them to the skin (refer to chapter 5, "Ways to Stay on the Scent").

• Have your essential oils within easy access and create a blend intuitively and quickly as you need it. A typical spur-of-the-moment perfume for sparking the fire in a lover would be:

Aphrodite's Jewels

Clary sage	3 drops
Ylang-ylang	2 drops
Rose otto	2 drops

• Oils commonly known for their aphrodisiac qualities include patchouli and ylang-ylang. Clary sage is known for its euphoric qualities.

• You will need a notebook to record your most special and favorite blends. It's easy to forget your creative formulations, so write them down. Even our ancestors wrote down their most magical and effective concoctions. This way you can re-create your special moments any time.

This Goes with That

Once you have discovered several favorite perfume blends, you will want to avoid having them clash with other aromatic preparations. Using accompanying skin care mixtures and toiletries to complement your perfume is called "layering."

You can actually create your own skin care and toiletries to complement your perfume simply by choosing one or two essential oils from your perfume blend to add to your normal regimen. For example, if two oils in your favorite perfume are neroli and rose, you could add one drop of rose to your facial moisturizer, one drop of neroli to your facial toner, one drop of rose to your deodorant, one drop of neroli to your hand cream, and so on. When you continually layer these scents, it deepens the sensory experience and qualities of your perfume.

5

Ways to Stay on the Scent

LIFE IS SOMETHING TO DO WHEN YOU CAN'T SLEEP.
—FRAN LEBOWITZ

ONCE YOU HAVE blended a perfume, there are any number of methods you can choose to transport its fragrance into the air. Here are eighteen ways to make your aromatic mark.

Eighteen Useful Ways to Employ Aromatherapy

MASSAGE OILS
Choose your blend carefully to suit the mood you want to create, the venue, and

your lover. Mix essential oils with jojoba or sweet almond oil. The blending proportions are a 1 to 10 ratio. For example, if you have 1 ounce of massage base oil, you will require 10 drops of essential oil.

Massaging essential oil into the skin is by far the most effective way to benefit from the healing qualities of the oil. Oils are taken up into the bloodstream after being absorbed via the hair follicle. The more surface area covered by lubricating and massaging the body, the better.

BATH OILS

Add 5 to 10 drops of your favorite blend to a warm (not hot) bath; vigorously agitate the water to disperse the molecules of oil, then sink in. Indulge, relax, and enjoy. Remember, you can soak at the beginning or end of a day!

ON THE NOSE

For those who don't have time to enjoy the luxury of a bath, don't despair. You can place 3 drops of your favorite aromatic blend on a clean cotton washcloth and rub your whole body with it. You can also place a facecloth over the drain in your shower and drop a few molecules of essential oil onto it. Breathe deeply as you enjoy the healing vapors.

VAPORIZERS

It is a real joy to watch the whole family participate in the wonderful ritual of vaporization. A different member of the family can be each evening's lamplighter, meandering through the rooms of the house lighting candles in the vaporizers to set a mood for everyone to enjoy.

In this aromatic ambience you can watch the quality of your family's communication improve. A ceramic unit designed specifically for vaporizing oils is probably the most effective way of diffusing essential oils in confined spaces. There are so many beautiful vaporizers available that you can choose a different shape and color for every room in the house.

Add a few drops of essential oil to the water

in the top of the vaporizer. Allow the fragrance to permeate the room. The number of drops of oil you use will depend on the size of the room. For an average-sized room, use 8 to 10 drops of oil on the surface of the water. Look for vaporizers that have large bowls to allow for longer burning without your having to keep an eye on the water levels. Use only high-quality candles that burn for extended periods of time and shed a minimum amount of carbon when lit.

INHALATIONS

This is a wonderful way to clear your head after a long day at the office (or simply to relieve the symptoms of a head cold). Fill a large bowl or basin with hot water. Add 4 drops of essential oil to the water and agitate the surface vigorously. Hold your head over the basin and drape a towel over your head and the water. Breathe in deeply through the nose and out through the mouth to clear your mind, or in through the mouth and out through the nose to cleanse your chest.

CANDLES

Don't be shy with candles—the more the better. Choose different colors to reflect your mood. Burn pink, purple, and violet candles for deep love; red and orange for erotic encounters; blue for peaceful relaxation; green for healing; yellow for easing mental frustrations; gold and silver for esoteric encounters; and white for cleansing and purifying. Try placing 10 drops of a favorite aromatic blend on a candle and then lighting it.

You can even learn how to make your own candles if the mood takes you, adding your own blends, seashells, glitter, dried flowers—whatever symbols reflect your mood and personality.

ROOM SPRAY

Room sprays offer an ideal way to cleanse and clear a room either before or after lovemaking. Fill a 4-ounce glass bottle with distilled or mineral water. Add 10 drops of an aromatic blend and shake well. Attach a spraying mister to the bottle. Lightly spray the room, including bed linen and curtains, and breathe in!

WOOD FIRE

Nature often acts as an aromancer, providing the naturally fresh, crisp aromas of eucalyptus, pine, and camphor wood. If you don't have spiced wood available for burning, add a few drops of essential oil blend to the kindling, and a few drops more to the logs. If you are spending time directly in front of the fire with a loved one, add a few drops of pine, cedarwood, or sandalwood to a teaspoon of water. Throw this on the burning fire.

SAUNAS

Saunas can provide the ideal space for cleansing the body, but we recommend that you NOT make love or perform any strenuous acts while taking a sauna or for thirty minutes afterward. The sauna can help you cleanse old energies and prepare you for the new. The ideal sauna blend is:

Hot and Steamy Blend

Eucalyptus	3 drops
Lemon	2 drops
Sage	3 drops

Add these 8 drops of oil to a ladle of water and splash it over the heated sauna stones. Never pour pure essential oils directly onto a flame.

FRAGRANCE BOWL

Add 10 to 12 drops of essential oil or a blend of your favorite oils to a small bowl of water and place on any warm surface—a gas or electric heater, radiator, etc. Take care that the water does not overheat, as this will diminish the oil's effectiveness.

CERAMIC RING

Attach an unglazed ceramic ring to the base of a lightbulb. When drops of essential oil are applied to the ring, the heat of the lightbulb will cause the oil to evaporate into the air. This is ideal for traveling, as the air in hotel rooms can be stale and musty and vaporizers are breakable and can become too sticky to pack.

POTPOURRI BOWLS

You can buy unscented potpourri in many stores and add to it your favorite aromatic blend. Stir the potpourri regularly to keep it fresh. Or dry and save the rosebuds your lover sends you and place them in a bowl. Add a few drops of rose otto to give them extra fragrance. If you're more the mountain-air type, gather pinecones, clean leaves, and wood chips next time you're out walking to make your own nature mix. Just add the appropriate aromatic blend to suit your mood.

PERFUME FOR THE SKIN OR HAIR

Wear an essential oil perfume on the wrists, ankles, and behind the ears. Rub some oil on your fingers and gently tussle them through your hair. Add an aromatic blend to your final hair rinse in the shower. Consider the Japanese geisha girl, who rubs essential oils through her pubic hair.

Tissue or Handkerchief

This is the simplest way to make your aromatic mark. Three drops of essential oil on a handkerchief or tissue in your handbag, desk drawer, or pocket will ensure your personal fragrance signature is noticed. Sniff the handkerchief when you need a pick-me-up during the day. The aroma on cotton or linen handkerchiefs will last longer than on paper tissues.

Lingerie

Place a hanky laced with essential oil into your lingerie drawer for a long-lasting effect. Alternatively, a few drops in the last rinse cycle of your wash will do the trick. A hanky impregnated with oils popped into the dryer with clothing will make your clothes smell fantastic.

Bed Linen

Place a potpourri bag with your favorite blend in the linen cupboard. For those special evenings, a few extra drops on satin pillowcases and sheets will set the mood. Essential oils easily wash out of clothing and bed linen, so don't worry about stains.

Soaps and Shampoos

Buy natural, neutral pH-balanced soaps from a health food store and add a few drops of your aromatic blend. All essential oils are naturally antiseptic and antibacterial to some degree, depending upon the oil, so you will truly be cleansing your body when you use them this way.

What Every Good Aromancer Should Know

- Set aside a special space for your aromatherapy blending.

- Make sure you're not interrupted when mixing or applying essential oils.

- Never use essential oils on the skin without diluting them first.

- Never use essential oils around the eyes.

- Avoid using citrus oils on the skin in the presence of ultraviolet light.

- Geranium and ylang-ylang are not to be used on red and inflamed skin.

- Rosemary should not be used on those who have epilepsy.

- Thyme oil should be used with caution around the mouth and genital area and near mucous membranes.

- Basil and marjoram should not be worn topically during the first three months of pregnancy.

- Store blends in dark bottles out of direct sunlight.

Bibliography

Denise Brown, *Aromatherapy—Headway Lifeguides Series,* Hodder & Stoughton, London (1993)

Nik Douglas and Penny Slinger, *Sexual Secrets,* Destiny Books, New York (1979)

Wayne Dyer, *You'll See It When You Believe It,* Random House, Sydney (1993)

Susanne Fischer-Rizzi, *Complete Aromatherapy Handbook,* Sterling Publishing Co., New York (1990)

The International Journal of Aromatherapy Vol.3 No.1.

Peter Koestanbaum, *Existential Sexuality—Choosing to Love,* Spectrum, New Jersey (1974)

Patricia Maybruck, Ph.D., *Romantic Dreams,* Pocket Books, New York (1991)

Anne Moir and David Jessel, *Brain Sex: The Real Difference Between Men and Women,* Mandarin, London (1989)

Leon Nacson, *A Dreamer's Guide to the Galaxy,* Nacson & Sons, Sydney (1994)

Alex F. Osborn, l.h.d., *Applied Imagination,* Charles Scribner's Sons, New York (1953)

Joan Radford, *The Complete Book of Family Aromatherapy,* Foulsham, Berkshire (1993)

Maggie Tisserand, *Aromatherapy for Lovers,* Thorsons, London (1993)

Judith White and Karen Day, *Aromatherapy for Scentual Awareness,* Nacson & Sons, Sydney (1992)

Judith White and Karen Day, *Scents and Sensuality,* Nacson & Sons, Sydney (1990)

Valerie Ann Worwood, *Aromantics,* Pan Books, Great Britain (1987)

About the Authors

Judith White and **Karen Downes** are experienced aromatherapists and health and lifestyle educators. Karen developed her skills in aromatherapy after a career in beauty therapy, while Judith's background includes bodywork and tactile therapy.

Both Judith and Karen studied holistic aromatherapy in Europe, the recognized center of knowledge in this field. As well as establishing busy aromatherapy practices in both Melbourne and Sydney, Australia, they have facilitated international distribution of the purest essential oils available in the world today.

Acknowledged as leaders in their field, Judith and Karen lecture and teach aromatherapy throughout the world, sharing their personal experiences and knowledge with tens of thousands of people and providing their audiences with tools to transform their lives.

Their first book, *Aromatherapy for Scentual Awareness,* is an international best-seller.

Leon Nacson was born in Alexandria, Egypt, to Greek parents. In 1952 he migrated to Australia, where he currently resides. He is the founder and publisher of *The Planet,* a newspaper that deals with issues of environment, health, and personal development. Leon is also the managing director of Nacson Promotions International, a visionary company that has facilitated seminars and workshops throughout Australia for such individuals as Deepak Chopra, Louise Hay, Shakti Gawain, Stuart Wilde, and Denise Linn. Nacson Promotions also publishes books on health and personal growth and has ten best-sellers to its credit.

If you enjoyed this book, look for *Aromatherapy for Scentual Awareness* at your local bookstore, or order it directly from the publisher. Send orders and inquiries to:

CROWN PUBLISHERS, INC.
C/O RANDOM HOUSE, INC.
400 HAHN ROAD
WESTMINSTER, MD 21157

For sales and title information you may call:

800-733-3000